Science Experiments

WITH

FORCES

Sally Nankivell-Aston
and Dorothy Jackson

W
FRANKLIN WATTS
LONDON • SYDNEY

This edition 2003

Franklin Watts
96 Leonard Street, London EC2A 4XD

Franklin Watts Australia
45-51 Huntley Street
Alexandria
NSW 2015

Copyright © Franklin Watts 2000

Series editor: Rachel Cooke
Designer: Mo Choy
Picture research: Susan Mennell
Photography: Ray Moller, unless
otherwise acknowledged

A CIP catalogue record for this book
is available from the British Library.

ISBN 0 7496 5337 X

Dewey Classification 537

Printed in Malaysia

Acknowledgements:
Cover: Steve Shott; Sally and Richard Greenhill pp.
7cr; Robert Harding Picture Library pp.4cl, 10br, 17tl,
23bl (Robert Brown), 27tr (G.M. Wilkins), 28tl (Geoff
Renner), 29tr (David Hunter); Image Bank pp. 5bl
(Robert Holland), 18cr (Ulf E. Wallin), 20br (Gianni
Cigolini); National Motor Museum, Beaulieu pp. 12br,
18bl; Science Photo Library pp.4tl (Claude Nuridsany
and Marie Perennou), 14bl (Mehau Kulyk), 25b.

Thanks, too, to our models: Troy Allick, Shaheen
Amirhosseini, Katie Appleby, Shaun Cook, Stacie
Damps, Stephanie Gharu, Gabrielle Locke and
Joe Wood.

Contents

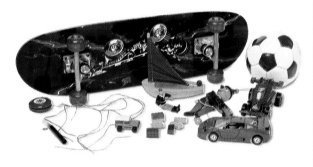

Forces all around

THE WORD FORCE IS USED TO MEAN different things in everyday language. Can you think of ways you might use the word? In science, a force is a push, a pull or a twist. You cannot see a force but can usually see the effect of a force (what a force can do).

Forces do all sorts of things. They can start an object moving, stop it, make it change direction, make it speed up or slow down and even change the shape of an object. There are forces acting on stationary objects, too! How are forces working in each of these pictures? Are they pushing or pulling?

Be amazed!

By doing the experiments in this book you can find out some amazing things about forces. You will find out about different types of forces and what happens when forces act on objects. Some experiments may answer questions that you already ask about forces. Some may make you think of more!

Look closely!

Scientists ask lots of questions and observe carefully, which includes feeling as well as looking. When you do the experiments, look closely and keep a record of your results. Don't be upset if your predictions aren't correct as scientists (and that includes you) learn a lot from unexpected results.

Be careful!

Always make sure an adult knows that you are doing an experiment. Ask for help if you need to cut things or stand on a chair or table. Be careful when you drop, hit or throw things and when you use elastic bands and springs. Follow the instructions carefully and remember – be a safe scientist!

Sorting forces

DO YOU REALISE HOW OFTEN you use push and pull forces in your daily life? Everyday activities such as getting dressed and playing with toys couldn't be done without using a force. Find out more in this first experiment.

1 Tie the two ends of each piece of string together to make three string circles. Label one 'Toys you push to move', label the second 'Toys you pull to move' and label the third 'Toys you push and pull to move'.

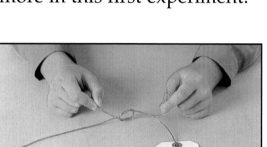

Keep thinking

All ball games involve using forces to make the ball move. Think of your favourite ball game. When do you use pushes on the ball? When do you use pulls?

2 Look closely at the collection of toys and place each one in the correct circle, or set.

3 Which set did you put the toy cars in to?

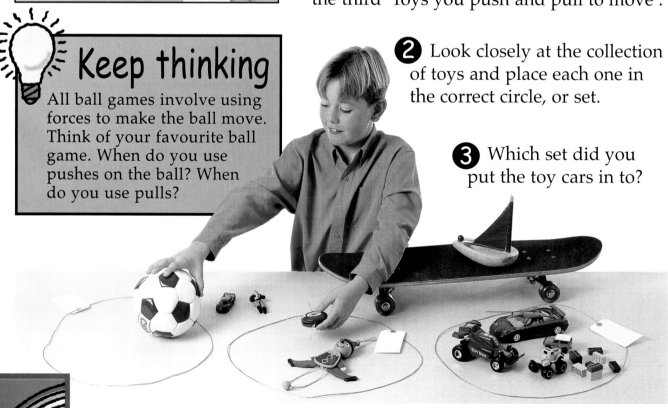

4 Take one of the cars. Think of different ways you could make it move.

5 Now try out your ideas. Did a push or pull force make it move more quickly?

6 Now find ways to slow it down, change direction, then stop. Were pushes or pulls acting on the car each time?

In action

Playgrounds have all sorts of activities which need pushes or pulls to make them go.

Don't stop there

● Take the sailing boat and put it in a sink or bowl full of water. Predict how you could make this toy go faster, slow down, stop and change direction. Try out your ideas. Did you use a push or a pull each time? What was making the push or pull?

● Ride on your skateboard. What safe ways can you find to go faster, slow down, stop or change direction?

Measuring forces

FORCES CAN BE LARGE, such as the force you use to lift a heavy suitcase, or small, such as the force you use to lift up a feather, or in between! Find out about different sized forces and how to measure them in this experiment.

✔ you will need
- ✔ a small box (e.g. a margarine container)
- ✔ 4 elastic bands (3 thin)
- ✔ 20 marbles
- ✔ ruler
- ✔ small spring (e.g. from a ballpoint pen)

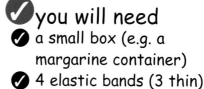

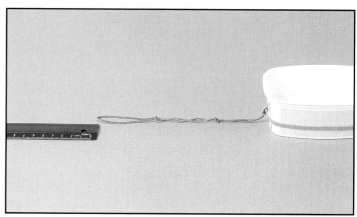

1 First stretch one elastic band around the box and join it on to a chain made from three elastic bands linked together as shown.

2 Put the box on a flat surface (not too smooth, e.g. a carpet) and place the ruler in front of it so that '0 mm' lines up with the loose end of the elastic band chain.

3 Put ten marbles inside the box and slowly pull the end of the elastic chain. As soon as the box begins to move, look at the ruler to see how far you have stretched the elastic. Make a note of the measurement.

4 Now add ten more marbles to the box. Will the elastic band chain stretch more or less when you pull this load? Repeat step 3 to find out.

5 When the elastic stretched a little you were using a small force, but when it stretched more you were using a bigger force. Do you need a bigger force to move ten marbles or twenty?

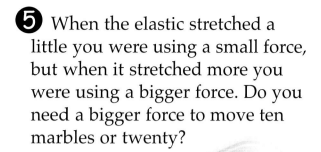

6 Now hook the small spring on to the elastic band around the box. Hold the end of the spring and pull the box of marbles. What happens to the spring?

Keep thinking

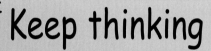

Look back to pages 4 and 5 to see large and small forces being used. Can you think of five more large forces and five more small ones?

Don't stop there

● Forces are measured on a force meter. A spring inside it stretches to show the size of a force, which is measured in units called newtons. Newtons are named after Isaac Newton, the famous scientist who studied forces in the 17th century. Use a force meter hooked on to your box of marbles to find out how many newtons of force you were using to pull 10, then 20, marbles.

● Put a 500 g packet of food into a small carrier bag and hang it on a force meter. Look closely at the scale on the meter. How many newtons are you using to lift 500 g? Can you work out how many newtons you would need to lift 100 g?

Feel the force

RUB YOUR HANDS TOGETHER. Can you feel the palms passing over each other? You are feeling friction. Friction is a type of force. Sometimes it is useful, but sometimes it is not. Find out more in this experiment.

1 Hold the skate and push it along a smooth floor surface. What does it feel like? Is it very easy, easy, hard or very hard to push?

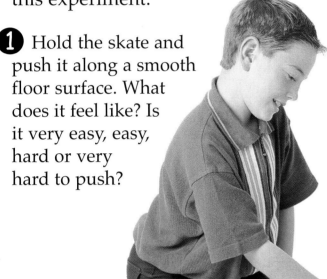

2 Now predict how it will feel to push the skate on four other types of surface, such as a wooden floor, carpet, thick rug and tiles.

In action

The surfaces on this skateboard ramp have to be kept smooth and free from stones so the skaters can move easily.

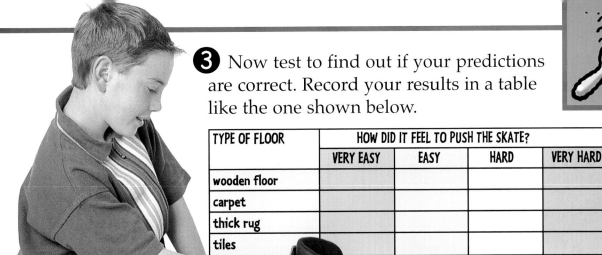

3 Now test to find out if your predictions are correct. Record your results in a table like the one shown below.

TYPE OF FLOOR	HOW DID IT FEEL TO PUSH THE SKATE?			
	VERY EASY	EASY	HARD	VERY HARD
wooden floor				
carpet				
thick rug				
tiles				

4 Which was the easiest surface to push the skate on? Which was the hardest? What differences do you notice between these surfaces? Why do you think some surfaces are harder to push on and other surfaces are easier?

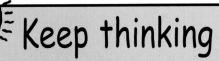

Keep thinking

What sort of force do you think friction is? Do you think it is a pushing or pulling force?

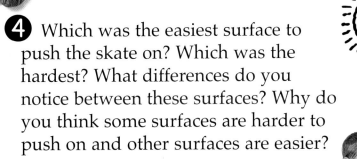

Don't stop there

● Put the skates on and go outside. Predict which surface will be easiest to skate on and which will be the hardest. Test to see if your predictions are correct. Is the smoothest surface always the easiest to skate on? Is the roughest surface always the hardest?

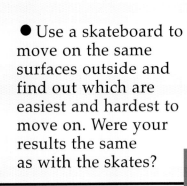

● Use a skateboard to move on the same surfaces outside and find out which are easiest and hardest to move on. Were your results the same as with the skates?

Get a grip!

WHEN HILL WALKERS CLIMB up steep hills they need boots with special soles to help them grip the ground. The friction between the sole of the climbing boots and the ground stops the walkers from slipping. Investigate the 'grippiness' of shoe soles with this experiment.

✔ you will need
- ✔ shoes with different types of sole (e.g. a trainer, a slipper, Wellington boot, school shoe, dancing shoe, party shoe)
- ✔ a force metre
- ✔ marbles
- ✔ weighing scales

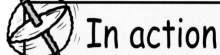

1 Look closely at the soles of the shoes. Predict which will be the best at gripping and which will be the worst. You can measure the 'grippiness' by finding out the force needed to start each shoe moving along a smooth surface.

In action

Tyres on vehicles need to grip well. Drivers have to make sure the tread on the tyres is not worn so the tyres can grip the road surface properly.

2 To make the test fair, you need all the shoes to weigh the same. To do this, weigh each shoe on the scales and then put marbles in each shoe as necessary. Tie string around each shoe.

3 Pull each shoe along a smooth surface using the force metre hooked on to the string. Record how much force is needed to start each shoe moving.

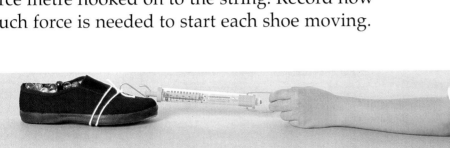

4 Which type of shoe needed the greatest force to start it moving? Line the shoes up in order of good to poor 'grippers'. Were your predictions correct?

5 What is the sole of the shoe like on the one that is best at gripping? What is the sole like on the worst one? Which shoe has the most amount of friction between the sole and the floor?

Don't stop there

● Repeat the experiment on a rough surface such as a carpet. Are the results the same or different?
● Repeat the test using a roller skate or skateboard. How much force did you need to move it – a large or small amount? Why do you think this is?

Keep thinking

Can you think of times when too much friction stops you moving in the way you want to? Look back at pages 10 and 11 to help you.

Pulling downwards

IF YOU HOLD A BALL in your hand then let it go it will fall downwards. This is because of the force of gravity, which pulls the ball towards the Earth. Do this experiment to find out more about how objects fall.

1 Look closely at the objects. Predict how each one will fall and land if you drop it.

2 Now test to find out if your predictions are correct. First, hold the tennis ball about a metre above a hard-surfaced floor. Drop it. How did it fall? Quickly or slowly? Straight down or in a different way? What happened when it reached the ground? Did it bounce?

Keep thinking

When you drop an object, two forces are acting on it – gravity and air resistance, the pushing force of the air. In which direction do you think gravity pulls and in which direction does air resistance push on the object?

3 Repeat the test on the other objects. Make sure you do the test in the same way to make it a fair test. Keep a record of your results.

4 Do all the objects fall to the ground in the same way? Do some travel more quickly than others? What force do you think is pulling the objects down to the ground? What force slows some objects down?

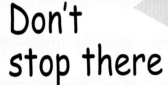

Don't stop there

● Screw up a piece of A4 paper into a ball. Predict how it will fall. Test to find out if it falls in the same way as a flat piece of A4 paper. Do they land at the same time? Why?
● Make a ball out of the modelling clay (about the same size as a ping-pong ball). Predict how the ping-pong ball and the ball of modelling clay will fall and land if you drop them together from the same height. Do you think they will land at the same time? Test to find out.

In action

There is no air on the Moon. When astronauts landed on the Moon they watched to see what happened when they dropped a hammer and a feather. The objects both reached the Moon's surface at the same time because there is no air resistance on the Moon.

Safe landing

HAVE YOU SEEN skydivers jump out of an aeroplane? Before they open their parachutes they fall very quickly, but as soon as the parachutes open they slow down. The canopies of the parachutes increase the amount of air resistance. Find out more in this experiment.

✓ you will need
- ✓ plastic bin liners
- ✓ 3 small toy figures of the same weight (e.g. Lego)
- ✓ ruler
- ✓ tape
- ✓ strong thread
- ✓ scissors
- ✓ a stopwatch
- ✓ a friend

1 Make three different sized parachutes by first cutting three squares from the plastic bags, measuring 20, 30 and 40 cm². These will form the canopies of the parachutes.

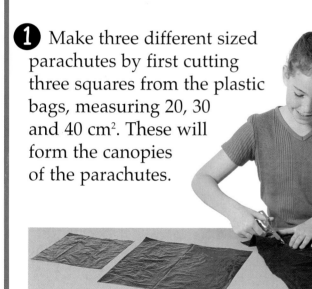

2 Then cut twelve 30 cm lengths of thread and tape a piece to every corner of each plastic square.

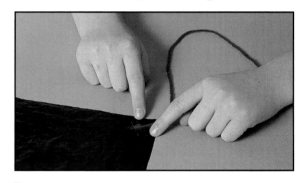

3 On each parachute, tie the four loose ends of thread together then tape to a toy figure.

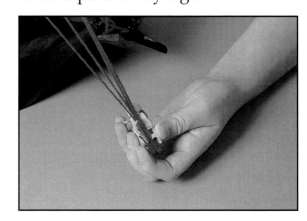

Keep thinking

The force of air resistance is a type of friction. Look back to pages 14 and 15 to find examples of other objects that are slowed down by air resistance. Can you think of other times when friction slows objects down?

In action

Even before they open their parachutes, skydivers spread out their arms and legs. This increases the amount of air resistance so they fall less quickly through the air.

4 Predict which parachute will be the fastest to travel to the ground and which will be the slowest.

5 Test to find out by standing on a chair or table (make sure an adult holds it steady) and throwing each parachute into the air in the same way each time. Ask a friend to time its journey from dropping to landing with a stopwatch.

6 Which parachute took the longest time? Which took the shortest? Why? Which parachute do you think would give the most comfortable journey and safest landing?

Don't stop there

● Make another 40 cm² parachute in the same way as before but this time use a larger figure (e.g. a Playmobil). Compare how this one falls with the 40 cm² parachute that has the smaller figure attached.

● Draw a picture of a parachute falling to the ground. Use arrows to show the direction in which the forces of gravity and air resistance are acting on the parachute.

Flying high

WHEN RACING CARS AND AEROPLANES move along, air resistance (sometimes called 'drag') slows them down. To reduce the amount that the air pushes against them, their shapes are specially designed to 'cut' through it. Find out more in this experiment.

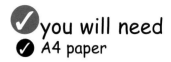 **you will need**
- A4 paper

1 Take one flat piece of A4 paper and predict how far it will travel if you try to launch it into the air. Test to see what happens.

In action

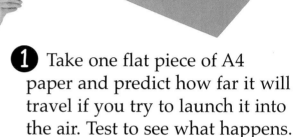

Aircraft like Concorde and these fighter planes are specially designed to 'cut' easily through the air. This helps them fly at huge speeds. We say that these shapes are streamlined.

Keep thinking

Like aircraft, land vehicles are also designed to reduce the drag. What features are on this car to help it cut through the air as it speeds along the road?

2 Now make a paper dart by first folding an A4 piece of paper in half lengthways.

3 Next make one end pointed by folding in both its corner flaps twice to the folded edge of the paper (see picture).

4 Fold in the corners a third time. Holding the dart at its centre fold, lift this new flap up to make the wings. Your paper dart is now ready to fly.

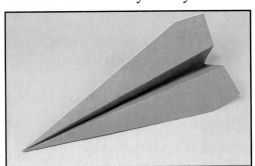

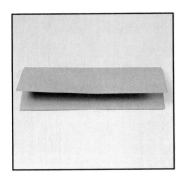

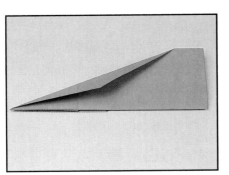

5 Predict how the dart will fly. Test to find out. Try launching it in different ways to get the best flight. Does it fly well? Is this a good shape for reducing air resistance?

Don't stop there

● Fix a paper clip to the front of your dart. Throw the dart. Does it fly better now? Why do you think the paper clip makes a difference?
● Hold a very large piece of card in front of you and run along a garden path or playground. Make sure you can see where you are going! Can you feel the air pushing against you?

Water pushes up

CAN YOU FLOAT IN A SWIMMING pool? Do you feel the water pushing you up? Find out more about the pushing force of water, or upthrust, with this experiment.

1 Blow up the balloon and tie it with a knot.

2 Hold the balloon over the bowl of water and slowly lower it on to the surface of the water. Do you think it will be easy to push the balloon into the water? Try to push it in a little way. Did it feel easy or hard? Gently let go of the balloon and watch what happens.

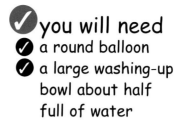

In action

These swimmers use the pushing up force of the water in order to float on the surface of the swimming pool.

3 Now push the balloon into the water again but this time push it down as far as it will go. Let it go and stand back! What happens? What force was pushing the balloon down into the water?

What was the opposite force pushing upward?

Keep thinking

In this experiment the water was pushing up the balloon. Look back to pages 16 and 17 to find out about another force that pushes up when something is being pulled down by gravity.

Don't stop there

● Take two equal sized pieces of modelling clay and make one into a ball and press the other one out flat. Hold them both on the surface of the water in the bowl and let them go at the same time. What happens? Did they both move in the same way? What force was slowing them down?

● Put some potatoes into a plastic bag. Make an elastic band 'handle' to the bag and, holding on to this, slowly lower the bag into the bowl of water.

Does the bag feel lighter in the air or in the water? What do you notice about the elastic band? What force is pulling the bag down? What force is pushing upwards?

Moving through water

BOATS AND SHIPS ARE designed to move through water but they are not all the same shape. Barges can be almost flat at the front, some inflatable boats are rounded and yachts have a pointed front. Find out more in this experiment.

✅ **you will need**
- ✅ 3 large rectangular aluminium food trays
- ✅ a piece of guttering with end stops about 1 m long
- ✅ 3 pieces of string or wool just over 75 cm long
- ✅ aluminium foil
- ✅ washers for weights
- ✅ sticky tape
- ✅ a stopwatch

1 First make three 'boats' with different shaped fronts. Fold foil around one tray to make a pointed front and around another to make a curved front. Leave one 'boat' as it is. Predict which boat will be fastest and which will be slowest.

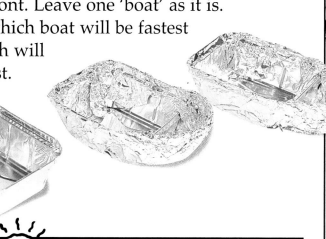

Keep thinking

Look back to pages 18 and 19. Is the shape that moves best through water similar to the paper dart shape that moved through air?

2 Tie a washer on to one end of each piece of string. Tape the other end to the inside front of each boat.

3 Put the guttering on a table with one end at the table's edge or overhanging it. Fill the guttering almost full of water.

4 Now hold one boat at one end of the guttering and hang the washer on the string over the opposite end. Let the boat go, so that the weight of the washer falling pulls it along. Use the stopwatch to time how long it takes the boat to reach the end of the gutter.

5 Test the other boats in the same way. Which one is fastest? Which one is slowest? Was your prediction correct?

In action

This surfer is on a board that is specially shaped to cut through the water so he can move very fast even though the water is pushing back against the board.

Don't stop there

● Draw a picture of one of the boats moving through the water. Draw one arrow to show the direction of the force pulling the boat along and another to show the direction of the water pushing against the boat.

● Try making a sail for each boat out of paper and a straw and stick them in with Blu-tack. Test your boats as before but move them along by blowing with a hand-held fan. Is the same boat fastest now?

Start, stop or change direction?

Hsnooker or pool? A forceAVE YOU EVER PLAYED
snooker or pool? A force
is acting every time the ball
starts to move, stops moving
or changes direction. Find out
more in this experiment.

✔ **you will need**
- ✔ a ping-pong ball
- ✔ a piece of thick card (about A3 size)
- ✔ a thick book

1 Put the book on a flat surface and lean the card against it to make a slope.

2 Hold the ping-pong ball at the top of the slope, let it go and watch it closely. What force do you think made it start to move? What force made it slow down and stop moving?

Keep thinking

Look back to pages 14 and 15. When you dropped the ping-pong ball, what did it do when it hit the ground? Why?

24

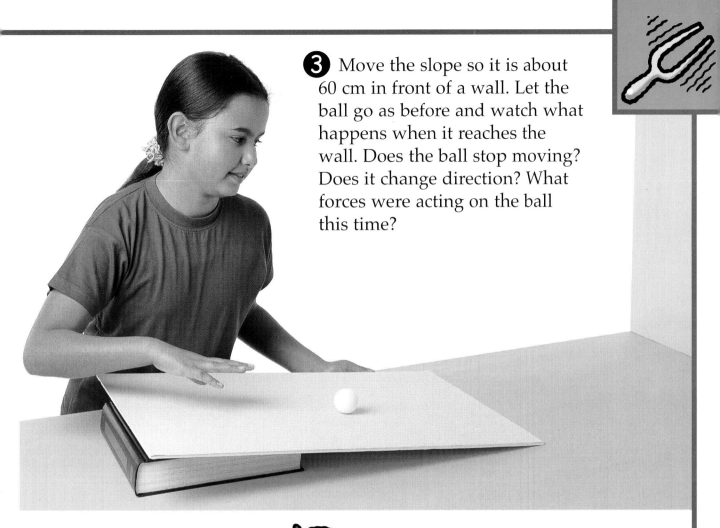

3 Move the slope so it is about 60 cm in front of a wall. Let the ball go as before and watch what happens when it reaches the wall. Does the ball stop moving? Does it change direction? What forces were acting on the ball this time?

 ## Don't stop there

- Draw a picture of the ball hitting the wall and add an arrow to show the direction the ball was moving before it hit. Draw in another arrow to show the opposite force (the wall pushing back on the ball).
- Hit a tennis ball with a racket against an outside wall. What happens when the ball reaches the wall? What forces are acting on the ball?

In action

Isaac Newton made many discoveries about forces. He was the first to suggest that the force of gravity existed. He also realised that a force is needed to start something moving, stop it moving or make something change direction. He called this idea his 'First Law of Motion'.

Changing shape

WHEN YOU PUSHED the balloon into the water on pages 20 and 21 did you notice that it changed shape? A push or a pull force is needed for something to change shape. This experiment uses pushes and pulls to make biscuits.

1 First wash your hands.

2 To make your biscuit mix, put all the ingredients into the bowl and mix together carefully with the fork. Use your hands to gather the mixture into one big ball.

3 Sprinkle a little flour on a table and make three golf-ball sized pieces of mixture and place a card on top of each piece.

Keep thinking

Look back to pages 14 and 15 when you dropped the ball of modelling clay. Did it change shape when it hit the floor? What force caused this?

4 Use your thumb to push down a little on the first ball, push down harder on the second one and push down very hard on the third one.

5 Take the cards off and look closely to see what has happened. Which one ball has changed shape the most – the one with the small, medium or large push? Which shape is best for a biscuit?

In action

You can use hard and soft forces to shape clay. This woman is modelling clay by gently pushing it with a tool.

Don't stop there

● Get some cake decorations or chocolate chips and press them into your biscuits. Do you need a small, medium or large push?

● Use the rest of the dough to make interestingly shaped biscuits with pushing and pulling forces. Make them all about the same thickness. Ask an adult to bake your biscuits in an oven for 45 minutes at 150°C (Gas mark 2, 300°F). Let the biscuits cool before you eat them!

Opposite forces

Have you ever seen a 'tug of war' game, with two teams pulling on a rope? The team which pulls with the greatest force wins the game. But what happens if they both pull with the same amount of force? When there is a push or pull force there is always an opposite force pushing or pulling back. Find out more in this experiment.

you will need
- a friend
- paper
- a pen

1 Sit at a table opposite your friend and both of you put your right elbow on the table and grasp each other's hand in an 'arm wrestling' position.

2 Ask your friend to push gently against your hand but do not push back. What happens to your arm?

3 What happens if you do push back and with a greater force?

This duck is floating on the water so the forces acting on it are equal.

4 Draw pictures using arrows to show the directions in which the forces are acting when you 'arm wrestle'. Use a long arrow to show the greater force and a shorter arrow to show the smaller force. What length arrows will you draw if the forces are the same?

Keep thinking

When an object is placed in water gravity pulls it down and the up-thrust of the water is the opposite force pushing it up. If the object floats these forces are equal. Which force is larger if the object sinks?

Don't stop there

Hold your palm flat and put an apple on it. Can you balance the force of gravity by pushing up on the apple the same amount as gravity is pulling it down?

Glossary

This glossary gives the meaning of each word as it is used in this book.

Air An invisible mixture of gases, including nitrogen and oxygen, that surrounds the Earth. People, animals and plants all need air to live.

Air resistance The friction force of the air that slows objects down as they travel through it.

Canopy The part of a parachute, usually made of some kind of cloth, that slows it down as it falls through the air.

Drag The pulling back force of air resistance that slows an object down as it moves through air. Drag pulls in the opposite direction to the one the object is moving in.

Experiment A fair test done to find out more about something or to answer a question. Sometimes called an investigation.

Fair test A scientific test to find an accurate result. To keep the test fair, when you are experimenting, only one part (variable) must be changed and all the other parts (variables) must stay the same.

First Law of Motion The scientific law first suggested by Isaac Newton that a force is needed to start an object moving, make it stop moving or to make it change direction. In science, a law is something that is always true.

Float To be supported by, or suspended in, a fluid such as water or air.

Force A force is a push, a pull or a twist. When a force acts on an object it makes it move, speed up, slow down, change direction or change shape.

Force meter A device with a spring inside it, which is used to measure force. The greater the force the more the spring stretches.

Friction A slowing down force that occurs when surfaces rub together.

Gravity An invisible force between objects. On Earth and the Moon it pulls objects down towards the ground.

Hand-held fan A battery operated fan that is held in the hand.

Launch To start something moving through the air, sometimes by throwing.

Load An object lifted or moved.

Moon The Moon is a vast ball of rock that orbits (circles) the Earth. We say it is a natural satellite.

Newton (N) The standard unit used to measure force, named after the scientist Isaac Newton.

Paper dart Paper folded into an arrow shape that will glide in the air when thrown.

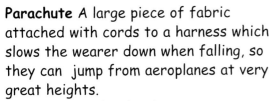

Parachute A large piece of fabric attached with cords to a harness which slows the wearer down when falling, so they can jump from aeroplanes at very great heights.

Pool See Snooker/pool.

Predict To suggest what will happen in an experiment before doing it.

Result(s) The outcome of an experiment.

Set A group of similar things.

Skydivers People who jump out of aeroplanes and use a parachute to land safely on the ground. Skydivers can jump from very great heights and free fall through the air for several minutes before they open their parachutes.

Snooker/pool Two similar games played on a table using a long stick (or cue) to knock various coloured balls into pockets placed around the edge of the table.

Sole The bottom of the shoe which shields the sole of the foot from the ground as you walk.

Spring A coiled piece of wire which can be stretched or compressed but returns to its original shape afterwards.

Stationary Something is stationary that is not moving.

Stopwatch A watch that can be used for timing how long something takes, measuring minutes and seconds very accurately.

Streamlined Specially shaped to cut through the air or water very easily.

Upthrust The upward push of water.

Washers Small flat rings often made from metal or rubber.

Winged seed A seed such as a sycamore or maple seed with 'wings' on it so it will be carried away from the tree by the wind.

Index